After I Was Dead

WITHDRAWN

After I Was Dead

*Poems by Laura Mullen*

THE UNIVERSITY OF GEORGIA PRESS
ATHENS AND LONDON

Published by the University of Georgia Press

Athens, Georgia 30602

© 1999 by Laura Mullen

Designed by Betty Palmer McDaniel

Set in 9.5 on 14 Optima by Betty Palmer McDaniel

Printed and bound by McNaughton & Gunn, Inc.

The paper in this book meets the guidelines for
permanence and durability of the Committee on
Production Guidelines for Book Longevity of the
Council on Library Resources.

Printed in the United States of America

03  02  01  00  99  P  5  4  3  2  1

Library of Congress Cataloging in Publication Data

Mullen, Laura, 1958–

After I was dead  :  poems  /  by Laura Mullen.

p.  cm. — (Contemporary poetry series)

ISBN 0-8203-2096-X (pbk.  :  alk. paper)

I. Title. II. Series : Contemporary poetry series

(University of Georgia Press)

PS3563.U3955A69    1999

811'.54—dc21                    98-36308

British Library Cataloging in Publication Data available

# Acknowledgments

Thanks to the editors of the following journals:

*Agni:* "House (Where the winds cross . . . )," "Secrets"

*The Alembic:* "Western Civ."

*American Letters and Commentary:* "Structures"

*Antæus:* "Appearances," "Drive"

*BOMB:* "Autumn," "Immigrations"

*Boston Literary Review:* "The Slave of Representations"

*Chain:* "35 ¹/₂"

*Colorado Review:* "The French Lesson"

*Denver Quarterly:* "A Little Blood," "Letter (Burnt)," "Self-Portrait as Somebody Else," "The Selected Letters"

*Exquisite Corpse:* "Mystery House"

*Lingo:* "White Paintings I–V"

*The New Yorker:* "House (Where it should have been . . . )"

*notas:* "The Self"

*Virginia Quarterly Review:* "Banyans"

*Volt:* "After I Was Dead," "For the Reader (Blank Book)," "Love Poem"

*And thanks and . . . —*

to Carole Maso and Carol Snow (you keep me alive)

The Karolyi Foundation and the MacDowell Colony

R.A., J.C., C.D., R.D., J.G., P.G., B.H., E.M.

Gerald Freund (in memory), and Joseph Lease

Marcus Pietrek and Robert Ryman

The Rona Jaffe Foundation

The National Endowment for the Arts

The *Denver Quarterly* for the Hull Prize

to *The love of my life.* . . .

*Given back to silence, this not-quite-open book*
*Is an open grave (though no one's): for the life I took.*

# Contents

After I Was Dead

# Banyans

The way they begin again
In the air is obscene:

The way they keep starting over—
*Reaching for, reaching for . . . —*
Adding on another version,
And then another.

Each one equally true in time,
Or so it would appear:
And all of them
True in the end,
Even the thinnest
Excuse, now—swaying and turning
In on itself in this light
Wind—left
Dangling,
Down at the end of a limb,
In thin air.

\*

(A map of our hungers,
Like the place mat, for tourists—
The deep, even, blue surrounding
This state pocked with enticements:
Oranges, rockets, half-naked girls—
We open the menu over.)

It shouldn't be this clear:
        Our need for each other.

\*

The way they begin again;
Not trusting the earth,
      Not trusting the air;
The way they keep asking
      *Is it, is it . . . :*
The way they keep starting over—
*Green* and *green* and *green*—
Wanting more.

\*

Dense and tangled:
The trial and trial and trial. . . .

\*

*I think there was something else*
*I wanted to say here. . . .*

\*

And is there a tree there, one tree,
Somewhere in the center?
Somewhere you could get to
With a sharp blade, a single
Tree lost in the forest of itself
Uncertainty conjures up,
Saying, *Maybe,*
*Not yet, And also, But if,* and
*Perhaps . . . ,*
Et cetera, et cetera?

\*

Not any version more or less true, however:
Only anterior.

\*

Imprisoned in its doubts—
"Empiricist!"—like a curse.
Poor tree,
Physician and invalid at once:
Afflicted with a "mysterious illness," and
Constantly coming back
For more tests.

\*

(As though the billowing green
Silken tent grew its own
Tethers, as though the swelling
Balloon gave birth to the intricate
System of ropes and weights keeping it
Pinned to the ground.)

An intelligence mad in its rigor,
Its rigorous doubts.

\*

Do I love you? Am I really
In love with you?
Yet? Enough? *Is this*
*What you were looking for,*
*Is this it?*

And the sight of them cut
By the side of the road,
Sickening: the deep
Entanglement, still
Writhing, cross-section,

The nest of snakes.

\*

To begin again—
Further out on a limb—
I can't bear it. Nothing
But rough drafts,
The lines left unfinished,
*Not forever.*

And the glossy leaves
Gleaming against the blue
Sky now,
*Not enough?*

(But the reason for this?)

(Freud, exasperated—
Stock still on the threshold—
Surrounded by journalists,
Raises his hands to his head,
*"All that matters is love and work!"* Words
Lost in the crowd
Of distrusts.)

\*

The tentative
Versions, beginnings (again), additions—
*No, wait, please, I'm sorry, I didn't mean to,*
*Let me explain*
*This*—tremble in place
Like the dangerous live
Wires the hurricane left
In its wake (signals
Stopped, the voices

Maybe went on, but in
Silence), in this
Breath of a wind,
In this breath. . . .

(And the earlier certainties twist, strain,
Caught in the trap they set.)

\*

But I can't
Finish this.

(Married over and over again,
As though that would help.)

\*

I wanted to grow
Out from the center, one
With myself: smooth
And singular,
As though I'd gotten it right
The first time,
Taking a shape
I could keep
Faith with. I had an idea
About destiny, fate, wholeness;
I wanted to have one
Uncomplicated desire:
To say *yes*
And to mean it,

Nothing held back.

*For once.*
*At last.*

Terrible to be so obvious.

\*

But just a choice,
And then another choice,

And then another after that?

The slender roots trailing out
        In mid-air,
Incoherent . . . —

Not to be able to stop this . . .

# Love Poem

A glimpse of you and then gone.

Boxes that tick.

Fling? Fling.

The word "just"
(Not as in fair, as in only:
As in *I was only . . .* ).

The lonely.

      Flung, as in violently—
*Hearts that tick*—
      Ulterior motives—
You saying that to me:
        "Ulterior motives."

The smoke from a candle
Blown out

Under a light spills
      Upward billowing
In on itself in the air as blood
      Pulled up from a vein
Through a needle
      Into another
Solution

Spills, billowing
Like smoke.

Layers of translucencies,
Then gone.

Or, just *invisible.*

Tick, tick.

As though another
Sheer floating veil or shroud
Of explanation could solve it.

Anything.

How they get delivered,
Ticking like that.

# House

*Where the winds cross*
*Where the currents meet*
      (This voice came to me)

House of wind or water
Shifting

Sliding in and out of

Shape. "I . . ."—
Where for an instant. . . .

*Where perhaps for an instant. . . .*


\*   \*   \*


And then I thought the warmth I felt, in the dark, clear, deep, bitterly salty and cold water—it went all the way down, this sudden warmth—was something dangerous: another body, resting on the bottom (waiting), or, because I knew by then the canal was polluted, some kind of toxic waste (I went that far, in my fear, yes) the edges of it (that heat) were so distinct. And knowing the fear was crazy, but not being able to shake it off—"probably crazy"—wanting out, and not even being sure the sensation was real (intense sensation that could have been pleasure, if I could have . . . ): not being sure I wasn't making it up.


\*   \*   \*

Voice which came out of the silence.

A "silence"

Held in place:
The sense of there being no place for anything other
Than the dutiful return
To the picturesque.

\* \* \*

The mountains on the other side,
Clear-cut.
Patches of thin green, new growth, and the three
New dark red gashes,
"We can't do anything about . . . ,"
A wave of the hand towards the view from the table,
"It's in another county."

Carried easily over the water all day the dense sound
Of gears changing to take the steep grade,
The trucks heavy.

\* \* \*

Intermittently,
Afloat,
Leaves, twigs, grasses;
The cobweb-fine meshes
Of bright green moss.

Near the shore
The white splotches of empty
Oyster shells gleaming up
From the bottom.

Four seals in the distance I was also
Frightened of.

(Changed, in my dream,
To four sharks—
Which *waited:*
Had *intention,* lurked. . . . )

But the scar across my ribs,
In the mirror, later, where I was
Peeling away the wet black suit,
Was a strip of seaweed, merely—
A fake wound—
Which also came off.


\* \* \*



House taking shape and collapsing.
"Not trustworthy."

                (That last the most constant
                Voice or the voice
                Most constantly trusted.)


\* \* \*

Not looking at the actual
Mountains (which had been
Spoiled) but at their
Reflections in the water,
Or learning to see them
As, at dusk,
Lovely shapes: violet-
Blue between the gold sunset
And the silver water.

Sheer mass we watched—our faces
Close to the glass to shadow
The mirroring window—a private
Display of fireworks
Burst out, show up, against.
In silence.
On that side it was night already.
But we had to look carefully, to keep
Our eyes lowered: the last
light above the jagged peaks
Still blinding.

\* \* \*

I wanted to stay,
Was trying to stay

(Up in the slight warmth of sunlight, merely: you could see, still,
    the whole
White length of arm and leg)

On or at least near
The surface:

*Careful. Good. Safe.*

The attention to beauty, to detail. Something
(Large) rotting away or wrong (waiting)
Underneath.


\* \* \*


Silence.
Or the voice that said Why live.

And the words drained of meaning,
Specifically "love."


\* \* \*


"Not trustworthy."


\* \* \*


Blues, greens, golds, and the light off the water
Imitating water
Across the red brick of the fireplace, the bare wooden walls:

A golden net, swaying, which dissolved
And lifted clear again, shifting, from moment to moment,
Never still. . . .

*Which faded away as the sun went down.*
*Which faded away slowly as the sun went down.*
*Which faded away,*
*Went out,*
*As night set in.*

The rhythms—
Found out in the effort
To fix it—so seductive: the illusion
Of something being prolonged or held back.

As if you could put it on "pause" forever,
Flickering slightly, but staying:

As if you could open up the instant before
And live there,

In the inevitably belated
*"As if it hadn't yet. . . ."*

As, for instance, with the accident. . . .

(But you pointed out how, in trying to locate it, whatever "before"
was [(that fault)], the place where it could have been halted or made
to happen differently, kept getting further and further away, kept go-
ing back, out of reach, like the roots of the horsetails, which had
"taken over": everything too entangled—a network—and going down
too deep.)

As, for instance. . . .

* * *

In the clear-cut beside the road—
Where the skid marks . . . —the shatterproof
Glass lay like blue ice, in summer, across the rough flesh-
Colored edge of a redwood stump, and sparkled among the dead
Branches and small broken trees which had been
Not worth it,
Evidently.

Darkness also
Slowly closing over that.

* * *

*But not a surface,*
*Unbroken;*
*Not a skin,*
*Closed off.*

* * *

I had a sense of things as fragile,
Myself as well;
*Threatened,* but also
Part of the threat.

A sense of things as held in place
With some effort: an agreement,

And an urgency to the pretence
Of there being nothing urgent.


\*  \*  \*


Up in the sunlight layer, buoyant, staying as close to the surface as I could get, I was still a moving break in the tension, I could tell, a hole (in that mirror), a gap, a betrayal, a dark place. Wondering what whatever it was that was at the bottom was reading me as. A shape. "Afraid."


\*  \*  \*


I got up and went for a walk
Along the narrow strip of beach the tide
Had given back. The rocky beach,
Littered with oysters and empty
Shells, a flowing line of leaves
And broken twigs, moss and grasses,
Running the length of it, high up
On the steep bank.  It was still
Very early—the light silvery, pale—
No one else up. I went out on the dock
And sat on the sprung diving board,
Looking out.

I was trying, this time, to get past
"Guilt," which wasn't enough, anymore,

Which was a way, I thought, of keeping
Something always between the actual
Event, and the image—
I was holding onto, of myself—

It shattered.

Oh, not exactly "perfect."
A laugh; the small waves, made up
Of wind and current, slapping lightly
At the dock, the reflections
Shifting, I'm not talking about that:

But I could see how I had managed,
By being "guilty," by my expressions
Of grief and shock and self-disgust,
To keep (the outlines
Rippled but inviolate) a sense of someone
"Good enough," or rather, "almost
Good enough"
To go on living.

(Someplace *distant.*)

But I could no longer afford
The cost of the two
Establishments. . . .

The picture
I had had to break
Myself
To keep intact.

\* \* \*


Maybe the dark
Green on the sides of the silvery
Waves was a chance to look in,
For once: the actual color;
The lid of a box, opening up
And shutting. . . .
A glimpse,
Borne towards me and swept past,
Of a possible house.

*(Long grasses swayed there gently,*
*Together and apart, the vacant*
*Shells glimmered up, bone white, and three*
*Crabs clung to a ragged shred of fish—*
*Each one frantic to both eat and keep*
*The thing—so that it fairly waltzed*
*Across the sand, the unwilling feast:*
*A jerky, halting dance, the gestures*
*Broken down into abrupt*
*Fragments. . . . )*

# Structures

"I" the poor glue.

And he was "very moved by those doorways
        he found in Tibet."
Which led into nothing and out of nothing.

Holding the disparate moments together,
Or separating them? Empty frames.

"The sequence exists when and because
        it can be given a name,
It unfolds as this process of naming takes place."

*Archways the sky showed through.*

Call me later.
Echoing off the invisible walls.
(Fear sets in.)

I felt like I had been broken open.
I said *God, oh, God,* but nothing
        stops time.

(A little false, a little stiff with each other.)
*(After.) (Before.)*

*Always the sky showed through,* the possible
        sky, on either side,

Courteous, disbelief to disbelief.
"That tree's kept its leaves for a long time."
(Already taken care of: put in a letter.)
But that vivid, sickening color only exists
        outside the body.

Was it revenge?

Fat gray cat named Guinevere nosing the garbage
        set out on the front porch.
(The descent, the betrayal.)
Was it the true
        love, the one you sleep through?

(To look in, to walk away.)
The chill damp mist, too pervasive
        to be "falling."
(To stand outside the lighted window and look in.)
The idea of myself I want to present to you.
Calling
        from "the pay phone on the corner."

In the rain. (Out in the.)

Just marking time.
The walls we would have had
        to imagine.

The walls, the windows, the doors:
"Why didn't you . . . ?"
"Why didn't you ever . . . ?"

Forcing myself to lean forward,
       to say it anyway.

"I" the thin
       ice on this river.

You would have to decide for yourself
       if you were walking *out* or *in.*

Was it the true
       love?

Brightly painted but "leading
       nowhere":
As the saying goes.

*Always the sky, that obscene*
       *innocence*
On either side.

(Thinking the rest of the prison
       into place.
Thinking hard.)

No marks on the body this time.
No clues.

# Appearances

In Baltimore they painted
Bricks to resemble bricks.
There too, I hesitated
Over the purchase of a deal
Wardrobe with mirror, papered
Over—I swear this—
With what seemed to be
A photograph of wood
Veneer for a veneer.
                              The thing
Gleamed slickly, and cost
Fifty dollars, and I left it
Where I saw it: in one of the thrift
Stores, down by the water,
Where the change
Was counted out by hands that shook.


\*


This was between the Salvation
Army and the projects; Church
Hospital and the porn theater.

HOT STEWARDESSES! BURNING
HIGH SCHOOL CHEERLEADERS!
The titles might have given rise to a fear
The place was a fire hazard,
But the few men leaving, one by one,
Hands in their pockets and eyes lowered,

Looked as gray and as cold as the salt
Water, sluggish and oily, in the harbor.
And the line forming down the block—
In the early dark—was outside
The mission, for a hot dinner.

*


Burnt out, falling down, boarded up,
Some of the houses seemed to have been
In a war, while others merely suffered
The effects of an easily manipulated desire
To have things be other than they are: veils
Of chicken wire, anchored to the brick,
Had been slathered with a heavy mixture
Of pulverized stone and concrete,
Shaped, then, into "stone" and "mortar."
No, not to be, but to look
Other: more solid? More expensive? Older?
The sense behind the gesture was by then
As long gone as those who convinced the owners
This was "the wave of the future."
                                    In the future
Which arrived, whoever could afford the labor
Blasted and chipped and scraped the false
Front off: the word then was the weight of it
Weakened the structure.

*


What I regret about that time
Is how good I was at convincing
Myself all I needed was the appearance

Of love, which might—so it seemed in my deep
Naïveté and cynicism—be all love was.
Whatever love is, it isn't
The thing I tried to will into being
Back then: like an unbroken sleep,
A smooth surface. . . .

What I like to think of is the *Pink Nude*
By Matisse, left to the city of Baltimore
By the Cone sisters, who left, as well,
The record the artist kept—in a series
Of photographs—of all the other paintings
This one could have been and briefly was
(The subject shifting slightly in each frame
As though restless). Up close you can see—
In the worked-over, punctured canvas—
The traces of everything it took
To come to this.

# House

Where it should have been there were only memories.
They liked it anyhow and lived there. For them
The moment it fell down was the moment it lifted up:
Livable-in at last.
A pantry full of regrets; a garden
Planned out in the shape of a plan, lush
With *what-might-have-been* and *O-if-only;*
A folly where . . . on fine afternoons. . . .
And the parties they threw there then, or rather,
Imagined themselves throwing, who had never been
Much for parties, but "Better late than . . ."—and the rest
Of the phrase lost in laughter. Love bloomed
In the nonexistent parlor: the piano
That never was was closed, suddenly,
By the woman who looked at her hands so as not to see
The face of the young man who knelt at her side,
Enrapt. Impossible ever to know
If it was the sunlight which had faded those curtains
So slowly that no one had seen, or whether
They had been wrong about the color from the start.

# Drive

There are signs we've memorized and when we work them
They work us. Think about it, you said, seriously—
Not meaning it. I think I'm not very patient—
I was coming to that. What's with this person
In front of me, I wonder, what's with this light. Shit.
For one terrible week I lost entirely my sense
Of where it started, where it stopped—my car—and I bashed
Small dents in both sides and lost one of the headlights.
There—I confessed. There are certain kinds of power,
You said, that make us powerless. I don't get it.
The freedom to follow the rules, you said,
And you laughed. Let them widen the causeway,
Then—my problems with intimacy are not entirely
My fault. Is *that* what you're driving at? What
Are you driving at? From here, you said,
To there—don't you wonder a little about. . . .
I said I *am*, laying on the horn a little, "enjoying
The process." Why, just to turn a corner, would
You need to hit the brakes much less stop
Almost completely? It's driving me nuts: I can't get
Here or get away from here fast enough,
It seems like. Our illusions, you muttered, darkly,
Our separate. . . . I just want to admit that rocketing
In front of that car going slow in the fast
Lane I think I'm *teaching* them something:
Look, I say, this is how you do it. Someday
I'll probably get shot. Meanwhile a kind of paralysis
Caused not so much by the terrible accident
We're all creeping up on now as by everyone
Slowing down as if to say, No, not me, not yet.

# Autumn

Her hair, brown.
Her speciality, damage.
Her specialty, becoming
Something else. Her hair, falling
Leaves, leaf rot, and then soil.
Her specialty, telling us
What we were trying to say
"All along." Her hair,
An introduction—our
Reading—her eyes also
Brown. Conclusion?
The jewelry sold by now.
Her hair, a phone call.
Is anyone home.
Gusts of cold wind
Shifting the leaves a little:
The leaves already married
To the ground. Her hair
The same color, sorrow;
Her sleep, long. I don't need
To tell you. The ground
Keeping her not so far
From the road. Her long
Hair, a transition.
She should have been
Somewhere else.
She should have been
Home. Her shoulders
And belly and throat
Beginning not to be

A secret any longer.
Whatever it was she was
Wearing, gone.
Her specialty, regret.
The skin, the definition
Of the bones. You know.
Her specialty, calculated
Indiscretions. Bothered
By all this activity, the birds
Are still. Was she meant
To be found? The hands
Holding nothing now.
Something has gotten at
Whatever was exposed. Her eyes,
Terror, and her mouth, hope.
We would prefer not to
Feel anything: to watch
As if from far away while
They try to make sense of it.
With one repeated phrase
They are taping the woods off:
"Do not cross." The trees
Are suddenly evidence.
Their specialty, containment.
Hers, regret.
We prefer to think of ourselves
As not restricted. Not like that.
Long arms flung out, holding
The "rocks and stones and trees."
Her hair and her eyes and her mouth
All a part of the ground.
Her specialty, being silent
"As the grave."
Our specialty, looking into it.

# The Selected Letters

Dear S.,

   How lovely you looked last night in that cocktail dress
We threw away years ago, gold or silver lamé, some metallic material,
Catching the light in the depths of the closet when I opened the door.
Buried (that self with the one who wore it, and the brief incandescent arc
Of "flinging her shoes into the sea") because I *felt* like it.

   And yes, I am willing to confess, finally, the most horrible things
About myself, but not in person; not—as they say—to your face.
But this salty liquid I dunk you in, darling, brings "the whole of it"
(O cherished phrase) back to me: the gin on your breath and the crash
Of the breakers, the wee hours and the victory already understood
As unbearable terror, a light not daylight seeping in around the edges
Of the scene . . . the slightly forced laughter, "but how drunk we
     were, dearest!"
How drunk we always, always were, and "the party"—sing along if you
     know this one—
"Never stopped."

   Now the *au jus* running down your chin (I think, "dribbling"?), how lovely;
And how did you smell? Just a little moldy, the faint scent of earth
And wood rot, you know, clinging to your skin (and your skin clinging . . . ).
There isn't anyone else I love as I love you, no one else
I'm so frightened I'll become. When we said goodbye at the wide metal gates
In the early morning, I thought, *I shall never love like this again,* and—
Just underneath that—*My body is full of worms.*

   Was it me you called your little one, your child? How could you desert me?
What am I but that now, or what am I? (Here where each image
Has its trusted, my-love-I-will-never-desert-you meaning.) An elaborate
Series of gestures? A code?

Dear S.,

   Last night when you said, but no, I can't repeat it . . . ;
But I wanted to lay you out, right there on the floor.
Too bad about all those other people. Still, the blond boy
Who chased you down the long hallway—clawing your back
And screaming "My little chickadee"— might have been me,
In a manner of speaking. Let's get together again sometime soon.
All this written to you from the edge of that pool, my darling,
Which hangs like a tempting jewel above the sea. From this side
Of the chain-link fence I can see *les autres;* describe them, cut up
Into diamond-shaped pieces, of course, on their side of it, but it is "safe"
To view them if your heart is less tender than mine. And *you* have no heart,
No heart, not "dancing, in a strapless gown," to the admiration of the waiters
Who pause mid-dash, fingers to lips, and sneak shy glances at each other.
No heart for the dirty green breakers and those who pass so briefly
Before them and are gone (my, my, this is poetry). I wish there was
    some way
To caress you properly, but my hands look so brutally ugly on your all-
But-unblemished skin. Well, this *is* just a note—they're closing
The club tonight early, you see . . . and "for good."


Dear S.,

   Lead and then concrete and still I wake up screaming. But then
I thought that special glow you had would animate the contents of a tomb.
Now this self-consciousness you've begun to evince appalls and frankly
Astounds me! (That's what I murmur, "Astounds me!"—trying it out,
With an expression of concerned reproach, in one of the fragments
Of mirror.) Must I return, again, to that party—the expensive gaiety of
    which has left all
But "my soul" in hock? Yet there is no other setting for you at once
    so artificial

And so true, that is, *realistic.* I'll fill in the details of your attire
Later (as if we couldn't guess them, down to the telltale shadows
Where the knife "entered repeatedly"), but when you dropped
Your long lace glove and let it fall—and when it fell, so slowly
(As if in a dream, *a guilty dream,* I thought it took years
To fall, "fluttering like a wounded . . . ," no, or, "flickering at the edge,"
That's closer)—and then deliberately looked away and let that young man,
Your "brave little soldier," bend down and use it to . . . —but no more.
*Je serai morte,* of course, sooner or later, then finish it
As you wish, or, in italics, <u>The manuscript breaks off here.</u>
(O, delicious self-pity, really better than that wedding cake
Of a white dress you wore.)


Dear S.,
    "I can barely stand to write you, tears spot the page,
The pen trembles in my hand . . ."—is this anything more
Than the coiling and uncoiling, in its viscous fluid, of the tapeworm
Which is my longing to tell a connected narrative so believable it ends
    up eating
Itself—"How could you, O, how *could* you?"—and choking—"When
    you know
How jealous I am," and how bestial, everything beautiful stained and torn
By the force of this ravenous hunger to "speak the whole truth and nothing
But the truth." And what gets left out or left over—the loathsome remains
Of the decayed feast with its delicate pattern of paw prints in the thick
    soft dust;
Its layers of silvery veils; its living lamé, feeding their way in deeper . . . —
Is "the rest," which, "is silence," silence: broken down, hacked up; silence.
And yet, *Often have I at waking found my fingers ringed with the long worms*
*Which bred in the corrupted flesh of my infant.* That ought to do it,
Don't you think? Now it's the closed door cutting off the roar of laughter

And you're hanging above the white porcelain bowl of the toilet,
Fecal stains and little hairs rampant, willing yourself to throw up.


Dear S.,
   I don't think I can go on being this honest much longer,
Already my imagination wears. I wish I were you, do I? Dead for a long time
Already, though I know you don't think so (but "gawd" I'm sick of the way
You pretend). And "Heavens!"—what a narrow spotlight
It is, after all—and then this crowd, "my dear, what a crush!" And what
Are the pains of my love to these horrors I can make up, I can never
   make anything up
To again. "O, the souls of the dead," and the bow drawn badly across
   the strings,
"The merry, merry . . ." and where did you get that queerly-shaped
   instrument?
God knows where it came from but I damaged it (skipping away with a
   shriek of glee).
And what I can accomplish here! Twist bodies, dissolve faces, finish off
The operation with my teeth—all while I'm sleeping, and the nightlight
Makes the closet suck the dark back in. When he smiled
I could see his eyeballs, they were lying on his tongue, he had a
   dazzling grin,
And he took off his hands as he came towards me . . . "You can't do
   that to people!"
*In the middle of the night, in one of those lonely places . . . —*
"Why can't I?" The pattern of flowers from their kimonos was
Burned into their skin.


Dear S.,
   Last night . . . —but perhaps it doesn't matter . . . —still I wanted to
   tell you . . . ,

And yet, can't it wait? Soon we will be together, "one" again,
I feel it, and I have made up a heaven for you, my darling,
A perfect silence or white space for which these words
Are the mere skin (I think I want to be always outside of, pleading,
"This time send an answer back quick to tell me you're willing to let me
See you again!"). I can see you, that is, I can picture you (frame
    you) reading
This note as though I were there: how your maid (of ambiguous origins)
Hands you the scented paper creased by vanished enfoldings, sign
Of "many rereadings, amendments, trepidations," and you,
At your vanity table (the kept pet and luxurious symbol
Of over two thousand years of culture), barely deign to receive it.
I don't want to go into the necessary (to my yearning) details: the light
That shimmers above your dress of reflected hungers, the flesh where
    already the dark
Print of my hand is beginning to fade—instead I want to drape around
    your shoulders the contents
Of this week's garbage: coffee grounds, grease-stained newspapers,
Rotten eggs and moldy tomato, digging down for the less identifiable,
    while you scream,
In a voice pitched high—for radar—*What, Valentine's Day again?!*


Dear S.,
    Is it over, is it over? I want it, so much, to be over. It's suddenly
Fall: leaves straggle down unannounced, sawing the air as though
    conducting
Vivaldi; it's sunny, then not; stray dogs and children are blown past
Equally—or, "snatched into view and removed,
For *randomness,* and *The impression of time
Passing.*" As if you could care about any of this! But I put the season's last
Roses (a throttled color, the heavy petals fallen shut
Again) in a jar, though you won't reach up to take them.

I would have had you burnt but I wanted my words in stone:
I wanted these gestures of tending . . . "the plot," as we call it—
The illness outlasting the body forever, going on and on and. . . .

   I've been reading a bit about Melville and so far the best part is this:
He writes to his brother (whom he doesn't know is already dead
Of brain fever—the mails are so slow) to tell him "composure of mind
Is everything." Delicious, huh? As of course it *is*. I've got some
Decisions to make, as usual, but you've never seen me like this:
The violence so quiet now, so contained. Still my hands
Are bloody. If there's anything left to say, write it down in a letter:
As Melville puts it, "a long one . . . and not full of nonsense like mine."


Dear S.,

   Again I must reproach you with your behavior; you are an atrocity
All by yourself, my little friend! You will say I am severe, but I am cut
Severely, made up of black velvet discreetly printed with violets, a single
White ribbon at the throat. There are so many editors of columns
For the heartsick better qualified to answer you than I:
"Do you want perfect memory?" "Have you ever killed anyone?"
And it's not the words, I swear, so much as the tone: importunate,
Half-regretful (but lit by that merciful vision of one who, in white,
Out on the green lawn, later, says *It feels like another life,
I don't remember . . .* )—and I cannot and dare not reply.
   Who will I speak to now at those terrible affairs of which you were
   so fond?
Who will top the wall with glass and name
The ferocious dogs whose hollow barking fills to the brim this dose
   of night
Frothing with visible stars? Who will pause between
The deeds of unthinkable evil to make certain we understand?
I think you are never so cruel as when you are generous—civilize me
All over again, please!

Dear S.,

   When you tried to show me what you had meant "all along" I confess
I didn't believe it. I said *It can't work like that*. Now I know.
So I took off my hands and face and picked up another long novel,
"After the wedding," I thought, "maybe then I could stand
To answer the phone . . ."—and to speak into it, saying words that
   "skin and film
The ulcerous place" I call my mind. But "What is thinking? How do
   I process
Information? What is existence?" and where *were* you? Now it's too late,
Do you understand? I have to refuse your titillating invitations,
And the knowledge you ordered for me (in both senses of the word).
I have to make your career for you now: put those huge green eyes
In the history books, smear that expanse of white flesh across the big
   screen. . . .
Because where it ends I become your *agent:* empty inside, dead,
   finished—
And grateful for your faith in me, more than you can know.

# The Self

Faceless and voiceless, busy constructing

Wretched in the mirror the body you twisted

To hide, in a harder and more precise

Light—the will's (nothing inside

*To put across* (in

Vision at halt: that landscape of black wire

"I can't 'pretend' any longer"—this

Slips out (from under

Music, this music: disjunct and sorry,

"Meant to tell you . . ."—but the meaning

Stage). Whispers

*The white precipitate bloom*

"A note from the seemingly

(Under-

*We were not*

White and fragile blank light of this

In early spring, fading—"another storm"

(Blurs.) Each "like"

Saves, *at the edges: fingers; teeth.* I was

"A note from the seemingly calm,"

Which would soon be over.

# Immigrations

The raft drifts.
You wanted us maybe
To stay in that half-baked
Democracy you were trying to cook
Up for us, constantly re-couped
Perhaps? Now the bodies turn,
Impassioned, restless,
In the tide's wash, beloved.
Now those of us
Not drowned are also
Half-baked.

I have a lot of idiotic thoughts.
Theories, rather.
I imagine torturing the torturers—
Which means *I've never been there,*
*So we never met, we couldn't have met.*
I imagine I hear the white
Salt closing all the avenues
Of thinking off. And my head
Ticks like a bomb, like a clock:
Ticks *like, like, like*—
It could blow us all up.

The raft keeps slipping
Over the waters, the would-be
Citizens keep slipping off.

*("There being no necessary connection*

Between the significance
Of an event and how it plays on the tube.")

The ocean goes on slurping at that trucked-in
Sand: shifting it, washing it, putting it back
In circulation, and on the Drive a drunk coed—
Wafted by in the back of a pickup—lifts
Her shirt and shows her tits to the tourists,
On a dare from the guy she half falls against
When the truck gets caught in traffic.
Queen of the parade of passing bodies
For a moment, shirt over her face, that anxious
Laughter floating off.

Holidays torn into confetti-like
Scraps. Blown up and raining down
On us. Mouths open, eyes shut
For the mercy. Interlude,
Hands cupped. Love
Evaporates. We're losing our customs.
What I did on my break.

The raft slides toward the inevitable
Turning back point on the boundary
Between conscious and unconscious.
The terms outdated. The analysis. The brain—
Also imagined—drying out. Of course I stink.
The simple, fervent wishes that got us into
This mess. And your recipes, your promises.

And whoever arrives intact
In the *new world* has to start there
A *new life*. Replacing each dead

Family member, beloved: collecting again
The full set. An "unconscious" pact made over
The feast of air and salt, I meant
*Despair* and *hope.* To zip the plastic
Names up over the lost and start fresh.
The abraded faces returning
In sleep.

You want us to go back,
Fine, we'll go back.

# The Slave of Representations

1.
Takes up where that voice left off, *aware of your expectations.*

Or the result is a flattered window
  (in which the frame or fame of these objects is only distorted,
  not lost).

Another maid-in-waiting to the latest realism had the opportunity
  to view the table from all its possible angles at once.

*No tears.*

Nothing there as yet but his imagination.

In which the work of the parasite is to enact the projected
  resentment of its host.

2.
"This will be the dining room."
The cage of concrete and two-by-fours.
Blueprints in the stiff breeze he unrolled for success.
Everything falling into place.
*Because I say so.*
The ongoing attempt to "play house."

But I like best the moment when (finished) he wipes the back of his hand
  across his mouth.

3.
In the center of the room is the waiting or writing, the real
    space I imagine being let into.

(The imagined walls.)

*To set the knives down at the edges, just so.*

(The shared joke.)

The clutch of emotions elects you (or so you interpret),
    but not to be "loved," not as you think to be loved.

Meaning, *this is where the dining room is going to be.*

When walking past the damaged ones we are not-damaged, not
    slumped in our filthy rags madly articulate asking for change.

            Of course there was some responsible
                figure, event, moment

(And so reeled from origin to origin thinking *What do I advertise?*),

                        some situation in which the correct
                (And hopefully violent?) elements of . . . —
                But you'd think this was *The Interpretation of Dreams.*

(Imagined wineglass and water glass, a constellation:
The bristle and gleam of tine and blade around each empty place.)

And, *if you can translate this you have failed to understand it . . . ?*

4.
Projected image of the woman on the wall.
"Nothing there as yet but his imagination."
The nurturing woman, the woman
  feeding and giving. . . .


Perspective lurching into everything. Drunk as usual.
He stepped out of the car (onto the front lawn) to throw up.

*"This is the dining room. . . ."*
This is where we'll eat, the dining room you imagined
(Finished) all around you, down to the knives and . . .
(Expecting what?).

5.
A blank space I'm writing into.
A blank space (I'm waiting) to shut me up.

Because I was suddenly not thinking but thinking of my performance
of that: "thinking," what he would see (and think of), looking at that,
so I was thinking of how to present it for him, "Woman Thinking," or
better, "Lovely Young Woman Thinking," and so I began to, you know,
emphasize the look of, my look of *concentration,* but not thinking,
really, of anything but that—so he had to ask me twice. . . .

And if they put the table and chairs in there, so what?
They eat in the kitchen—separately, hurriedly—standing up.

# For the Reader (Blank Book)

The man in the white room next door wrote this, I think: wrote this thinking I wanted to read it. Our identical rooms pressed up against each other like the pages of a shut book. One of those blank books so popular a while ago and still, The Nothing Book. *Put your thoughts here.* And whether they were laid to rest or came to life hardly mattered, all a part of the cure. The one dream he'll write in his, over and over, is of waking early or being woken early by the wife he doesn't have when the light is strange. Something he thought he killed, she calls to him, is moving awkwardly across the lawn to the edge of the lawn: the blood an oily smear of almost black against all that crisp, evenly clipped blue-green. He lingers morbidly over description, oh yes, in what he likes to call my dream. At the edge of the lawn: woods or water; some kind of menacing refuge, something he'll never feel safe from. Dragging its limbs, the thing, mindless determination, making its slow way back in. Left here to get well some time ago, we are jolted back into all the attendant symptoms by the rare visits of those who left us, who come back to check in, *Can we stop paying now?* "For the settlers the wilderness seemed desolate and evil, something it was necessary to both cultivate and tame." *If you won't play the piano for me,* the guy in the movie we gather to watch in the rec room yells, suddenly, *you won't ever play it for anyone again,* and the cripple's cane comes smashing, on both fingers and keys, down. Ka-*boom.* We twine hands in the dark and promise to show each other everything, later. We promise we're going to say, this time, only what we meant. What an awful noise, the wife he swears he doesn't have sighs, again, but louder. What's *she* trying to recover from? "We would not have survived without the help of our mortal enemies." I dream I'm a pilgrim. I dream I'm knocking on the door just to the right of mine, which might in fact be mine, like the one to the right of that, they are all so remarkably the same, very late or very early, in one of the long white nights or mornings. *Is it over?* Her voice caught deep in his throat, the woman in his dreams says It isn't dead yet darling, you didn't kill it, you only maimed it darling, see, it's still moving. How long is it going to haunt him, I wonder, looking down from above at that plot of cleared land, what little we'd been able to make sense of.

# Western Civ.
### For the Mice

1.
I can't go into the kitchen for fear of disturbing them at their feast.

Each sound attaining new
Meanings.

Are they dying behind the walls yet?
Are they dying on the roof? Where
Are they dying?

(Still air inside the cupboard
Warm and fetid as a breath.)

Are they decaying as sound "decays": in a linear
Narrative, in a "progress"?

Because I can't see it.

I *have* thought.

Will they come out and teach me
Something about this
Dying, will I find out?

Too late? (*As always,* too late?)

Something somebody said once
Set out appetizingly, in a torn box

(That hot, light, greeny-blue—the pellets—
To what does their vision turn it?): something
About there being something
After this . . . —
*Something else.*

(Beyond regret?)

What?

(I wait and watch.)

I wait—*alone*
*And far from you—*
And watch.

2.
What do I want?
Not to have accomplished
What I set out

To accomplish?

To have been the agent
Of nothing, really,
*Intolerance:* just a little,

As we say, "fed up"?

Easy to talk
Of the bad taste left
In *my* mouth.

3.
"They have eaten all of the poison and gnawed
On the box, frustrated:
Wanting more death, feeling
They haven't yet had enough
Death."

Oh, they wanted it all right: rushing towards—
Fighting for—their punishment,
And yet?

It's a cheap trick.

"I threw the empty poison container away,
Half afraid they might seek it,
Even empty, in the garbage: so great
Is their lust."

It's a cheap trick to turn a hunger to this.

(I *know* that. But.)

4.
Do they turn upon each other
In the dark—as we did darling—is there
Some dim sense of fault?
Do they need that? Can they afford it?
Are they frightened, does it hurt?
Can you keep the wall from turning
To glass, and looking glass: leave some corner
Of the building dark, respect
The difference? Where they are dying,
As we say, "like rats"—

Can you manage that?
Because no matter how close you get

To understanding—sticking your fingers
Down your throat as though to eat
Yourself, trying to call back up
The food you wanted so much
To refuse in the first place: trying to make yourself
Thin enough to fit the enigmatic
Space behind the walls or under the roof
*(Come out, come out . . . )*—

They will not hurt less,
Or live for one more second.

(But you struggle alone with your conscience.
Isn't that great.)

5.
You probably didn't know what I meant.

Probably not.
Probably not.

I meant a bad job:
The blade dull,
The head crushed.

And then the invention of speech.

6.
(But the sticky pages left open
And waiting stayed blank.)

On one of these (failures) a lonely
Sign set down in the field of light—

The blue-green only slightly dulled
By its passage through the absent . . . —

A bitter laugh. You still don't get it.

7.
They came out for me,
Finally, oh yes—
Sick with what I'd given them
To eat—but they didn't
Die; or they didn't die
Fast enough: trapped
Between broom and dustpan,
As in an awkward parenthesis,
And dropped into the toilet, to be
Hauled away in the water's grasp.
Still "lively." Desperate. How
Small they became there,
And yet my feelings were not
Tender. Only, I was horrified
By this, by my . . . *capabilities*
Shall we say? The present
Seemed endless: there wasn't,
Apparently, anything else
But this. . . .

8.
The dust-colored bodies of time's
Secret agents. *Squeak, squeak, squeak.*
These professors finding their way

To the heart of the dry
Subject at last: footnoting toothmarks.
The torn-open, ragged subject,
The empty subject, death itself?

Or something (pause)
Like death itself?

That stack of memoranda—
"You like to call your unhappiness . . ."
*(Hurry, hurry)*—famous for its music's finished
Elegance. . . . These crrriiitics . . . :

Are they nibbling the edges?
Are they making it worthless?

*What happened*
*To the movement?*

Trapped in the forest which turns and looks back.

9.
(And then I began to see how it could be
A kind of insanity: yes, a *mad* voice,
And me listening to that.)
                              Walking back
From the party: the conversations
Breaking up into sentences, words,
And then nothing, but I was thinking
I felt almost human for once—
Since we talked.

Should I tell you that?

Should I try to tell you that?
Across the "necessary" distance?

10.
The curator explained
The stack of T-shirts (white
Lettering on black, "Always
A Bride, / Never a Bridesmaid"—
A thin gold ring stitched
To the cloth) were not
For sale, but the trace
Of an ongoing project:
A woman, "marrying
And divorcing as many
People as possible."
I think she said "people."
(And then—behind her hand—
Hissed, "I think conceptual art
Has gone as far as it can.")
But my parents, I laughed,
With their several marriages,
Hadn't known it was art . . . :
I just wanted one, to try
To wear the meaning out.

11.
Listen, darling . . . —
I was seeing myself like that:
*Waiting for the crumbs,*
*Hiding in the dark.* . . . I thought I was
Dying, yes, and that that sound I was hearing was also
The sound of my teeth . . . —at the edges
Of the apparent domestic

Success: controlled space not, obviously,
So well defended at night.
(They got in, meaning out
Of place.) *Longing for death?* What
Dreams I had! "Darling." And for months
Something moving out of sight
Just out of sight (my turning and turning
To look too late). *Jealous?* I was haunted by what
Could have happened and hadn't, or had,
But I'd missed it. Or I was missing it. Now. And the house
Like some wretched zoo or laboratory: stinking
Of cages and experiments.


## Epilogue (The Tent)

How the whole
Structure vanished or became
Something else.

What was that dream we had?

*Heal thyself? Come back*
*Up? And walk?*

So that:

Poison seeping into the very
Pages of the books.

Colorless, odorless. . . .

What was that dream we had?

(Drifting past—homeless—at night.)

*Whatever the cost?*

Dark blue against the dark blue
Sky the fastened plastic—billowing—
As though inside something struggled,
Still, to lift or escape.

*What was that dream we had?*

Somewhere a light left on: softly glowing
Place in the heart of the almost invisible shape.

And the signs posted warning us off.

I was (outside) seeing
This (because inside was death).

"The war had just ended, and I was trying to forget."

Coming back in the daylight: dry
Sound of the skins undone sliding down
The apparently unchanged
White side of the house—*time passes*—
The workers, in their other language,
Calling out, and that blue pouring down
To wad in stilled waves at our feet.

*We stopped for a while, and went on in silence.*

"Today," blank sheet, shaking hand, "we go back."
The last entry: "To what?"

# Mystery House

My Joke, my efflorescent ex-
Travaganza, please another bathroom
For the mad king of Bavaria. *Nothing
Is coming to an end, alas, dream on.*
I crushed the orders in my hand:
I had a fist, now what to do with it?
I dreamt you were fucking a chocolate cake
Beside a large window, curtains open;
"Oh, this hole is so tiny," you said. Please,
Another room for the ghosts of the victims
Of gunshots—they must be confused
Now they're dead by the vastnesses
Of the sad widow's mansion: these useless
Stairs going nowhere; doors opening
On nothing; guilty corridors that dead-
End. Oh my punch line! My cancerous
Structure! To divide *is* to conquer! I dreamt
I was opening boxes of funeral chocolates
From Vietnam. Sweets for the ancestors,
For the dead, who like that junk,
Damaged in transit, the creams oozing,
Mashed against the lid. You like it. I mean,
The window in the lid. I was trying to frame
A letter to those who'd gone before,
Who'd hired me, but how to put it? Please:
Another mirror-lined hallway, spare no expense!
We must show this unexpectedly heavy
Deluge back to itself. We must be
Prepared for the eventualities. These stained-

Glass doors never opened on the end
Of the family: the part that collapsed
Was abandoned, but construction
Only halted when the widow's heart
Stopped its fear-struck, guilt-struck
Hammering. Tell me how do you write
To the dust? Oh my very unfunny! At *"Flores
Por los Muertos"* we let the orchid rot
In its see-thru coffin while we defoliated ourselves
Of our *feelings,* feet deep in torn-up notes.
Please. Another turn in these stairs, another
Brick wall or glass ceiling, false alarm, set of bars
Across these bulletproof windows: they're clever,
The dead, hunger makes them
Clever, and they have nothing
To do but watch and wait.

# Secrets

They were "warehousing" all the empty apartments here, and now
The building echoes, empty, with the sound
Of the roller as the painter paints
The hallway, with the sound of the heels and toes
Of their shoes when they come to measure the windows,
Of their tap on the door when they tap on the door to come in
And measure the windows and take—sooner or later—
These windows I like so much away. The new ones,
I imagine, will be simpler and harder to open
From outside. They won't show me the outside
Cut into so many even pieces, each framed
In white . . . —I stopped there for a moment, held
Back (but you can't see it on the page), as if by bars,
When I saw that the easiest, best image—still—
For that was something I'd said before, used before; twice.
Now I can't be sure I'm being honest anymore. Or I have to
Let stand as the sign for being honest this effort to give it "all"
Away. Just the first effect of history. Having drinks
One night with my lover and a colleague the latter
Asked me how many men I thought I had slept with,
Right there, like that. We were drinking a lot and later I knew I, at least,
Was drinking too much. But I said I'd stopped
Counting a long time ago, and I meant it. And then he said
Roughly, and I said Forget it, and then he told us
How he counted the women up, at night, in the dark, like sheep.
His wife was away doing graduate work. What's the point of this,
What's the point of "all this"? Somewhere up there I was thinking—
It could have been the second line—*The need for money, the need for sex;*
Something I'd decided not to say (I couldn't see how it fit)

67

Finally got said, or was being said the whole time, or came out. Not all
The apartments here are empty. There's someone living
Next door I've never seen I know is there because I've seen
The small bags of garbage he or she puts out in the hallway
When it's late, when it's too late to go all the way out.
At the top of one bag the dried, curled-back-down-as-in-birth, dead
Ferns from a florist's arrangement stuck out, and a glass
Bottle. If I was ready to really look through it I bet I could
Tell you a lot about that person, I bet I could learn a lot
(But not as much as someone learned, whoever it was, hungry,
Who went through the garbage outside and found and ate the stale
Remains of my birthday cake, leaving behind the torn-open, empty box, not
As much as that . . . ). *The need to eat* comes under the heading of money,
*The need to know* comes under the heading of sex. Are you reading this
To find out something? Did you find it out? It's been on the market for years,
But now that the building's been sold and they're making improvements
Those empty apartments must be worth a lot, or they ought to
Be able to ask a lot, to get a lot for those apartments
Whose doors swing open on brightly lit nothing to the curious touch.
Even in this section of the city the new disease has emptied out.

# The War

1.
The light from the screen
Makes my eyes water. I'm taking
These notes in some
Exhaustion and pain. I think
If you freed my arms I could write
Better, I think I could write
Better if you paid off my debts
And dragged me a little closer
To the mirror, better yet if you'd teach me
Something about all these bankruptcy
Proceedings, better still
If you'd only redeem what's left
Of my feet. These are not empty
Promises.

I could run after you screaming.

2.
Am I ever going to finish
Trying to explain? "These shoes
Need to kick somebody," or "I don't exist
When you forget me"? All my resources
Have been exhausted! What do you *want*
It to mean? I believe if you loosened these
Bindings I could give you a better picture
Of what I hope to get away with here calling
*The sea.* Is this a *family resemblance?*
Where's the sunscreen? Who I am

When I'm not with you, I mean:
"I'm fighting my own particular war
With nature"? But I'm not a Nature
Poet! "Obviously." Leaves.


3.
There isn't any time left
In which to accomplish anything.
It feels like. What's this space
To be used for? It feels so empty. Is it
Empty because I don't love poetry?
Enough, I mean. Am I just—uncertain fingers—
Trying to gain access again
To my credit rating? Am I deserving?
What kinds of plastic do you take?
Stop kicking me. Then take off
The sign that says *Stop*
*Kicking me.*


4.
Comes back in. "Where's my chemical
Warfare, goddamnit, where's my enemy?"
"Asleep." "Asleep?" "Well, it's the middle
Of the night." It *is* the middle
Of the night. You there,
I thought I told you to leave that line
Of trees: meant to be a kind of screen
Seen through here to the bare
Earth churned up around the tilted
Stumps and blasted saplings half sunk
In a red and motionless sea. See?
What did I tell you? Branches and leavings.

5.

From a letter: "The war
Happens all around us, faithfully, without us
Really having to do much of anything, it seems.
It all gets done somehow." Leaving us feeling
Incredibly lazy? Past tense or *de trop?*
It's just a memory. We've been out-
Living.

6.

Leaving the redwood forest he made believe
They couldn't wait: pretending to drive away—
Actually out of sight, dust settling back on the dirt
Roadway and trees—with the rest of the family.

7.

It's just a memory. Of her desire
For money he said she was,
"Sticking a knife in my gut
And twisting it." He pantomimed
The gesture for his young
Audience, staggering back to fall
Against the cutting block. We were all
In the kitchen. He was obviously
Exhausted and in pain, fists
At his stomach as though trying to turn
A knife or a key. With some difficulty.

Which war do you mean?

8.

Downwind of the plant

When the valve blew. Removed
From active duty. The flutter of green.
"It's an ill wind. . . ." Finding it difficult
To breathe. Leaves.
Trips to the city. Remembering
Those who used to say sometimes,
"It isn't any good here,
Your money."

9.

Passed out in the shade
Of an empty shopping cart at the side
Of an alley, one of the guards
Catching a little shut eye?
One of the casualties?
One of the warning signs?
One of the many. I think
I'm forgetting how to read.
From a letter: "We don't even have to lift
A finger." Dust-colored clothes, the body
Apparently sinking into the ground.
One of the deserving?

10.

I think I could please you more
If you would untie me. I think I would be
Even more servile, if anything, if I were
Free. I promise this time. It might be the moving
Darker areas on the screen: making my eyes. . . .

11.

My hands are tied, really.

12.
I mean what other markets could I hope to open
So late in the game? I think I've proved I'm willing
To let you inspect my facilities. Each
Accommodation equipped
With hot and cold running wa . . . —
All the necessities. So why does it still
Feel so empty? Is it because I'm faking
Belief? He might be directing
The loading, remembering
How they can suddenly turn in the hold
And crush a man: the cut
Trees. In the middle of the night:
A couple of the guys slightly drunk,
Everyone else just tired and clumsy,
And the boat tied up at the dock,
Like a cradle, rocking and rocking. . . .
The air bitter cold, dense with salt, stopped
In your throat as though you'd been sobbing.

13.
Where's that music coming from?
I think I could write better if you fed me.

# The French Lesson

He's looking for the woman. What woman? The woman.
This country is rapidly becoming industrialized.

We're going out, he doesn't lie, she's punishing herself,
He's serving, you succeed, he feels bad,

When you go out. How is the weather?
It's lovely. It's hot. It's cold (chilly, etc.).

What is the subject of this comedy? He's a man
Who likes to listen to himself talk. Almost without

Wanting to, this means, like the other time,
The whole day long, beautiful horses, his (or her)

Beautiful hair. These things have nonetheless
A natural value. When he was young, he used to sell

Newspapers. Crocodiles used to be (formerly were)
Abundant (used to flourish). He was repeating: "Facts

Are facts." What facts? He is calling, his name is,
Very useful, every day, every two days,

He no longer brings, we were alone, his merit. He
Enjoys the respect of his friends. They aren't speaking.

He's calling Henry. His name is Henry.
In Memphis one finds temples where they were adored.

He nonetheless left (has left). Moreover, she remained
(Has remained). We fell (have fallen). Fortunately,

He did not fall. Toward the end his talk became obscure.
She set her glass down suddenly. He talked so much

That his listeners left toward the end of his speech.
She looked away. They wanted to leave early.

[The implication here, by the choice of the compound past tense as
opposed to the imperfect, is that they did indeed leave early; i.e., the
action was completed. Contrast *Ils voulaient partir de bonne heure* =
They wanted to leave early, where there is no such indication of
completion or realization of desire; all we know is that they wanted
to, we don't know whether they did in fact leave early.]

In the above experiments light acted as a chemical agent.
When I entered (went in, came in) they were playing

Cards. We are ambitious but we are also tired.

# 35 ¹/₂

Is this turning all too easily, too swiftly into
Language? A man keeps stepping out
From behind a banyan tree
Saying "Believe
It or not. . . ." Stopping. Starting over again. Stopping.

Of course there's a camera.

Of course there's a camera-
Man making it into
A movie, or trying: stopping
The speaker from stepping out
Of the frame, sending him back to "Believe . . ."
And the tree,
And the moving away from the tree.

What does the tree feel? What does the camera
Think about this? It's a fund-raising movie, "Believe
It or not, last year we were ranked in . . ."—
*You don't want to hear this.* I got out
Of there fast. "And so": the scene's stopped.

Incongruous, in a suit and a tie—stopped again
Mid-gesture, emphatic, between the tree's
Green and the lawn's—there's some guy walking out
Of a day in Spring (making a special pitch to the camera's
Potentially vast and yet intimate audience) and into
Something like timelessness. It's a matter of belief.
Or beliefs? That banyan's true, but hard to believe

In, in that dense cluster of trunks it hasn't stopped
Adding all those very slightly differing versions onto,
Like a news feed: tree, tree, tree, et cetera—
A dark mass of leaves above the whole business—the camera
Keeps running. *Don't worry, we can edit it out.*

I got out and I didn't get out . . . :
Like him I was getting paid to act like I believed
In what I was selling, only language was the camera
(So I was both of them) I couldn't stop—I couldn't stop
This I, I, I—turning into the tree
Now (do you *believe* that?), turning into

Something outside, stopped. . . .

Which goes on soliciting belief. For how long? O Tree,
O Camera. Just a couple of seconds turning into

# Self-Portrait as Somebody Else

Did it better: pathetic in the bathtub, post-
Water. Naked victim of what? In the late
20th century style: hurt-dirty, rage-
Soaked. Language running out, time itself
Just the remembered echo of a choking
Noise from the hole past history's hair-nested
Grate hard water's turned white. Hard luck.
Written out in layers, like music, the dead
Residue—*ash* gray at the reach, or *smoke*—
Begins where it ends: under the over-
Flow vent's chrome cover, the name
Brand of the fixtures apparently forever
Stamped into my distorted, weeping, slightly
Rust-rotten features. And I might be the Nazi
Industrialist's bride, or daughter; bleached
Whale in an equally creamy container, or an-
Other by-product of this over-produced self-
Portraiture, leaving a little something sticky
And stuck here even now (date expired),
Like a long-gone breath still ghosting a mirror,
Unable to come any cleaner, or closer. Seen
Under the scribbled list of greenish figures
Must totals on the tear-stained plastic curtain
Of this theater, I'm the remainder—a bit
Player; a black box cracked among fractions
Of landing gear, scattered; a mess of master-
Pieces in the *œuvre* of over; fetal in the after-
Math of the orders ("Happily"), feigning death

In the ditch of my life ("ever after")—until flesh
Scorched by cold takes me out of the picture,
Fear the already damp cloth in whose folds
Fading day sulks, guilt the expensive soap.

# After I Was Dead

I had time to think about things,
Time for regrets, like.
The glowing vessel of frozen booze
Lists: *Way a minit: wanna . . . 'scuss shumsing!*
Memory overflowing its salt-rimmed dike?
But your version only, "the" truth . . . —

Sliced. Time folds in on itself: bed to couch.
The sheets (to the wind) come clean:
I gave the keys back.
Comes (in hot water) the stain of love, out.
Comes nobody back from the said, *I mean . . . ,*
To say what lies still under all that black

(Ashes cling): nobody, that is, you'd trust.
I sifted myself, things over between us.

# White Paintings I

My lips are zippered shut.
I need distracting.
I've changed my mind: my face
Is boarded up like a house.
I'm nailed shut, it's got to be
"Like" something. Like life
Is happening and not happening—
Is happening too slowly
And too fast, because you can't
Stop it. You see your hands
Coming off the wheel, trying
To put something in between
Your face and your fate and
You hear yourself screaming.
What was it you heard yourself
Singing? *How did* "I" *get here?*
The force of the impact
Slammed us together. In school
We had a little song, we lined up
Neatly. In the open mouths
Someone dropped a coin.
Some coins. Breaking my fists
On this glass and then asphalt there is no
History, I said, meaning I don't want
To be touched. Now you've closed
The eye-flaps, you must want
Forgiveness. These layers
Are great: this white, off-white
And off-off-white in a dense

Application, but I feel like the latex
Is tearing. I hear the sirens—
*Please don't try to move me—*
I'm tasting the metal teeth: admitting
Everything's finished between us,
Or nearly, singing it over the rim
Of the lifted glass, mouth full of belated
Apologies; a clear fluid—spilling back out
Through the seams *(Completely,* you said,
*Untranslatable)*—escaping.

# White Paintings II

*(in parenthesis)*

So what if I scar?
I get my skin to yield up its secrets.
I know how everything is
Inside: suspended, contingent.
I take the knowledgeable risk.
I follow the loop to the final
Destination. I come again
To the part
Where I'm making the first
Cut, where I'm breaking
And entering,
Where I'm walking in
And taking the gloves off.
I watch it like a film.
Quiet in the audience.
I like these marks. Each time
Could be the first, if only
I didn't keep track, if only
There wasn't always more
Resistance in the surface
Where the badly healed
Silence twists in broken
Lines, livid and thick.
It seems that everything
Depends on something else:
It seems that everything
Wants out. It's a system.
So it hurts. I'm not surprised

I try to escape. Room
To move is room
To flee in, or
*All movement is flight.*
It's a system. It just takes time
To get used to it. I like to watch
The thing in action. Lights.
Camera. That first cut. I love it
When I squirm like that—
I'm all over these sheets—
But I'm disappointed,
Too. What can I say?
I expected more of myself.
*All movement is attempted*
*Flight, and useless.*
This is what happens, I say,
Trying to shove it all back
In some kind of order, trying
To remember how everything
Went *before*—positioned
In reference—looking for some
Epiphany to liberate, to take
Away on parole, at least:
This is what happens to you
When you don't cooperate;
This is what happens to you
When you refuse to talk.

# White Paintings III

Another funeral.
The glare from the open
Coffin throwing the mourners'
Shadows onto that shifting wall
Of insects so we are
Embroidered on the night.
They seethe, we seethe.
You no longer move at all
Insofar as we understand
Movement. Light
Seeping out like milk: the light
At least, escaping. To begin
With guilt. The faces of the other
Mourners tense—past
And present "relationships,"
Lips moving, voices lost,
Wondering just how long . . . —
Reflecting my own face?
To start over again, sorry.
This summer-weight
Black wool soaked through,
The sour river-scented
Air sluggishly swaying
These broken-off
Green threads the sick weeping
Willow's hanging onto
"For dear life"?
It isn't so late as all that,
Though we're, most of us,

By now, more than half
Memory, scrambled and
Unquiet (buzz, buzz),
Trying to weave you—
Stiff and unworkable—
Back in or at least mend
The tear in the fabric.
We know by now there isn't
Going to be enough
Time to finish it.
The wavering drone
Of these voices not
The music you wanted—
That doesn't exist yet.

# White Paintings IV
*(Independence Day)*

## 1.

Above the banks of fog the muffled thud
Of rockets—I remember—never seen,
But we stood there for a while, e*n famille*, looking up
At nothing. Intermittently brightening
And dimming, blank blanket above an airport
Built to test the instruments and abilities
Of those attempting to take off, or land, in this—
Thick whitish, murky soup, confusion—sightless.
Thud. Thud. Like something dead
Still being kicked. I don't need to add
What I add: *hollow, meaningless.* We piled
Back into the car and probably
Our father drove us home again,
If he wasn't already blind drunk.

## 2.

The unbroken wall of your silence, behind which: ghosts
And shadows, thin shapes in constant, shifting, flight;
The most intense of intimacies and then complete
Absence. . . . Unable to tell you even the first thing about it:
How I was out in the garden of ashes, the garden I painted
Completely white in the middle of summer, the garden of doors
Going nowhere, brought out of doors to be painted
And taken back into the house untouched because I never
Got around to it, not in time for the celebration; how I found myself
Out of doors in the sticky heat, one of the "grown-ups,"
In the green depths of a garden I'd only imagined

Painting white, I'd named "of ashes," drinking *blanc de blancs*
Until there were two of each guest I tried to make
Merge when they were speaking, carefully shutting one painted
Eyelid . . . ; how the voices seemed to come from far away
And stay there . . . —I have no memory of what we talked about.

# White Paintings V

I put my hands through your head.
But you never offered me
Any resistance. I put my arms
Through your body. I end up
Holding myself. I say *Somebody*
*Please get me through this*
*Part*—as though it were only a part. You
Disperse. You always disperse.
I walk through *You* like a doorway
In a structure made entirely of fog,
Set out on the edge of a cliff. "Falling
In love again . . ."? I walk in and out
Of us both. The letters I start
Break off, start over *(Somebody,*
*Please . . . )*, accumulate, becoming a body
Of work, aborted: fetus and corpse.
I try to read everything I possibly can
Into the silences: to see—
For "next time"—how it's my fault.
Where was the railing? The warning
Sign? The flimsy excuse? This stuff
Can't be grasped. I'm trying to tell you
Exactly what it's like to be this
Lonely and frightened. I put my face
Through your face. On this side
It seems our eyes are wet—
But that doesn't change anything.
Our "grief"? Even that will get
Taken apart. The walls of the building

Are covered with advertisements
For everything I ever thought
I wanted: in the shredded white
Skin sloughing off I still make out
The stuttered remains of wild
Suggestions and pleas, desperate
Ideas about happiness. I try
To re-imagine myself, free at last
Of your interpretations. I put
My hand out into the empty
Space it seems your hand could be,
If only I were somebody else: it fits
'Like a glove,' like it was made for me.
I put my fist through the glass.

# A Little Blood

Appears at the base of the nail. Torn
Flesh. Like the edge of a brilliant
Slip. Ragged how it seems or seeps.
Gathering to drop. Where someone
(I am gone now) halted: that border—
Where the unevenly mirrored *U*
Of the teeth met—*scarred* stiff. "I do not,"
I wrote, "forgive them for their silence,"
Earlier. For pretending, I elaborated,
I do not exist. My "flesh." I am far away
And still the spreading area or evidence,
Left unsaid, smarts. Who was so careless
As that? Not wanting to answer
I answered. Finger to lips.

# Letter (Burnt)

To plunge my fingers in the silky pile
Of ashes            again:
           That wish.
*Now.*            *Too late.*


      "Dear. . . ."    The pale field the rain
Leaves pockmarked.
             My hands as if gloved in it,
      Grayish. *Dear*
*Ghost.* Webbed in the skin where time underlines
And crosses out.      Now.   On the body
      Confessed.    Again in this:
I looked.      (The movement
      Suggested on the surface where the drifts
Shift: claw, to fist, to flat
             sweep—
      Close
To that game of three gestures, "paper" here meaning
*Release*).


      A light wind that won't lift the wet
           clumps. *Dear*
*Revenant.*


I start over again. "Dear . . ." I start—
      Trace.
The fire long out.
        I keep trying to read amid what—
      Charred to velvet—falls

*Fragile*                    Apart. A moment.
                    On my knees at the cold hearth.
But I can't make the words out.


"Dear . . ."—
                    Up to the elbows as if off to the opera in dust.
                         I unfold the delicate wings of a guess: smoke-
Darkened and stiff.
                    Like a jet wire meant
          To tear flesh:
The script. Rusted in place.   And broken off.
          Ash
                    Clouding the air where I clap
As if to free myself of this. That. Jealous
          Wish. I forget how to talk.


After how many years—
          X—
The wire parts. I forget
I forgot.                    My hands lost
          In the light
                    froth of soot floating up, I mimic
My own known gesture: to wash.


          "Dear . . . ,"
And "seemed endless," and "less and less," and "if."
I mouth,
                    I wish. *Dear*
*What.*
          And listen as the proof collapses,
Soundless.                    Breathe the rough
                    Draft—
Given or having taken there

Embodiment—to scatter what I search.

(As surf

From some far

Storm suspected: the past

Splashes over the present　　or is it

The future　　　　　　rushing the rocky outreach

Of the past—sends a spume aloft—?)　　(I forget.)

The wires,

Sharp-edged, cease: swift

Shapes

In nothingness sketched.　　What I think

When I think,

*I know*

*What I've lost.*　　Almost

weightless.

The fire out.　　The dead

Cinders sifted, swept, and

Then

Attended to a faithful

Representation　　of a former state

Of neglect, I applaud

Again away the evidence

Of my work: swirls

A dusky winding cloth sheer down the white

Walls of the sink.　　　　In this wish.

Whatever can't be brushed off.

Rearranged to look "untouched."

All the signs of the effort to complete

What would have been to come from what was left

Of us:


"Dear. . . ."

In the ashes the damp

Apparition of a circle—slightly
　　　Hardened—marking
Where each drop
　　　Hit, I lifted to extinguish
　　　　In my fist:
　To set down
　　　As smoke,
As salt.

# Reverences

*Hurricane Andrew;* Herbert Bayer & Roland Barthes; Wordsworth via Hass; "Monk" Lewis, *Hamlet,* & *Hiroshima;* the raft builders, the writers; Loyola, David Hockney, Michael Serres, Proust via Rapaport, also the architect & the editor; John Cheever & Gregory Peck; "Decon," Maude Gonne, Pound, Baudelaire, Alex Lambert & Eliot ("The Waste Land"); The Winchester Mystery House & *A Streetcar Named Desire;* Berryman via Clover; you, Hole *(Live Through This);* Eric Rhein.

# The Contemporary Poetry Series
## Edited by Paul Zimmer

# The Contemporary Poetry Series
## Edited by Bin Ramke

Christopher Davis, *The Patriot*
Juan Delgado, *Green Web*
Wayne Dodd, *Echoes of the Unspoken*
Wayne Dodd, *Sometimes Music Rises*
Joseph Duemer, *Customs*
Candice Favilla, *Cups*
Casey Finch, *Harming Others*
Norman Finkelstein, *Restless Messengers*
Dennis Finnell, *Belovèd Beast*
Karen Fish, *The Cedar Canoe*
Albert Goldbarth, *Heaven and Earth: A Cosmology*
Pamela Gross, *Birds of the Night Sky/Stars of the Field*
Kathleen Halme, *Every Substance Clothed*
Jonathan Holden, *American Gothic*
Paul Hoover, *Viridian*
Austin Hummell, *The Fugitive Kind*
Claudia Keelan, *The Secularist*
Maurice Kilwein Guevara, *Postmortem*
Caroline Knox, *To Newfoundland*
Steve Kronen, *Empirical Evidence*
Patrick Lawler, *A Drowning Man Is Never Tall Enough*
Sydney Lea, *No Sign*
Jeanne Lebow, *The Outlaw James Copeland and the Champion-Belted Empress*
Phillis Levin, *Temples and Fields*
Gary Margolis, *Falling Awake*
Mark McMorris, *The Black Reeds*
Jacqueline Osherow, *Conversations with Survivors*
Jacqueline Osherow, *Looking for Angels in New York*
Tracy Philpot, *Incorrect Distances*
Donald Revell, *The Gaza of Winter*
Martha Ronk, *Eyetrouble*
Martha Clare Ronk, *Desire in L.A.*
Aleda Shirley, *Chinese Architecture*
Pamela Stewart, *The Red Window*
Susan Stewart, *The Hive*
Terese Svoboda, *All Aberration*
Terese Svoboda, *Mere Mortals*
Lee Upton, *Approximate Darling*
Arthur Vogelsang, *Twentieth Century Women*
Sidney Wade, *Empty Sleeves*
Marjorie Welish, *Casting Sequences*
Susan Wheeler, *Bag 'o' Diamonds*
C. D. Wright, *String Light*
Katayoon Zandvakili, *Deer Table Legs*